Mobil New Zealand Nature Series
COMMON BIRDS IN NEW ZEALAND

Black Shag

Mobil New Zealand Nature Series
COMMON BIRDS IN NEW ZEALAND 2

MOUNTAIN, BUSH AND SHORE BIRDS

Janet Marshall
F. C. Kinsky
C. J. R. Robertson

REED

First published 1973
Reprinted 1975, 1978, 1980, 1982

A. H. & A. W. REED LTD
68-74 Kingsford-Smith Street, Wellington 3
2 Aquatic Drive, Frenchs Forest, NSW 2086
also
16-18 Beresford Street, Auckland
85 Thackeray Street, Christchurch 2

ISBN 0 589 00759 9

Phototypesetting by John van Hulst Ltd, Wellington
Printed by Kyodo-Shing Loong Printing Industries Pte Ltd,
Singapore

Contents

Foreword

The first volume in this work dealt with the birds of town, pasture and freshwater and included a large proportion of species introduced from Britain, Australia and elsewhere which play a prominent part in the modified habitats of modern New Zealand. The present volume, in contrast, deals with a wide range of native birds of the least modified New Zealand environments and includes only one introduced species (Eastern Rosella).

Open coasts and harbours,the remaining areas of native forest or "bush", and the mountains that form the backbone of the land support a diverse assemblage of bird species, in addition to many of those illustrated in volume one that penetrate far from town and pasture. The inclusion of several distinctive birds of freshwater lake and pond, riverbed and mountain torrent, links the two volumes. Together they provide an unequalled coverage of all the birds likely to be seen, in pocket-sized format to fit the motorist's glovebox.

New Zealand's biological individuality springs from a long history as an isolated archipelago and the birds in this volume span the whole spectrum of this history. Royal Spoonbill and Black-fronted Dotterel are newcomers from Australia that first colonised New Zealand during my lifetime. Others have been here much longer, including the distinctive Blue Duck, Wrybill, parrots (Kea and Kaka) and Tui, with no close relatives we can recognise overseas. The New Zealand Wrens are even more notable, forming (like the New Zealand Thrushes and Wattle-birds, alas no longer common, if not extinct) distinctive "endemic" families confined to New Zealand, which have been here for many millions of years. Finally the Kiwi, adopted as a national emblem, probably dates from the time New Zealand formed part of a southern continent, Gondwanaland, a hundred million years ago.

When we recall that in Great Britain and Japan (for example) the birdlife contains no ancient elements, no distinctive species older than the ice ages of the last million years, the special character of New Zealand's birds can be appreciated. It gives ample scientific or intellectual basis for the conservationist's plea that our distinctive native birds deserve special care. Our most interesting birds are often the least successful biologically and thus most in need of preservation. Some have already disappeared or are rare; long may the survivors remain common.

C. A. Fleming, KBE, OBE, BA, DSc, FRS, FRSNZ, FMANZ

Introduction

This volume, the second of two on the common or commonly seen birds of New Zealand, is not designed as a field guide or a text book, but for use in practical visual identification. The object, as in Volume One, has been through colour portraits of each species to give a visual image, complemented by a brief summary of information designed more as an incentive for further interest and study, rather than an exhaustive reference.

The species shown here are by no means entirely confined to *Mountain, Bush and Shore* habitats, but consist mainly of native and endemic species prominent in those parts of the country least directly modified by man. Many are secretive and confined to the generally more inaccessible parts of the country. Some may in fact be unknown to many people except through books. Compared with the urban areas and their more commonly seen introduced birds, the wide expanses of mountains, bush and shore may at first sight seem completely deserted. The secretive nature of many of the species may give an impression of a lack of numbers which can only be dispelled by closer observation.

The policy of milling native forest and its replacement by the more prolific exotics endangers the habitat of many bush species and regrettably the small and often discontinuous reservations of original bush are often related rather more to economics than the ecological requirements of birds and trees.

Unfortunately, the true numbers and habits of many of our native birds are relatively unknown. The result is public debate on conservation issues based often more on emotion than fact. In many cases the birds used as arguments for preservation of an area have been so affected by other factors that the preservation or removal of bush or wetland may have little effect on them. However, when sufficient facts have been available or obtained, previously unsuspected areas of importance have been revealed and subsequently reserved.

Thus with the growing interest and demand for conservation a knowledge of what is there or has happened is the first step towards the action required for a national policy in future. We hope that both at home and while travelling these two volumes will stimulate your interest and improve your understanding. All birds have their place and importance, let us conserve and enjoy what we have, regardless of sentiment and without differentiation.

Notes on Text

The birds appear in the same order as in the **Annotated Checklist of the Birds of New Zealand** except where two species are shown on one plate. Common, scientific and where available Maori names are shown according to the **Checklist.**

Species are divided into four categories:

Endemic — confined solely to the New Zealand region.

Native — naturally occurring in New Zealand, but also found elsewhere in the world.

Introduced — introduced by human agency.

Migrant — breeding overseas, but regularly migrating to New Zealand for part of the non-breeding season.

Scientific names are the only certain way of referring to any bird, as common names so often vary throughout the country and may be shared by several species.

Though we have tried to use simple language for all descriptions, an occasional specific term has been used.

Male — ♂   Female — ♀

BROWN KIWI

Brown Kiwi

(Kiwi)

Apteryx australis

Family: APTERYGIDAE

Endemic: Three sub-species. North Island (shown in plate), South Island and Stewart Island. (Fully protected).

Field Characters:
- —size of large domestic fowl.
- —loose, coarse bristly feathers.
- —long thin bill with nostrils at tip.
- —flightless, remnants of wings concealed in plumage.
- —moves about only at night, hidden in burrows during day.
- —Voice: an often repeated shrill whistle "ki-weee" in male, hoarse and lower pitched in female.
- —*North Island:* darkest and smallest, dark legs.
- —*South Island:* lighter and softer plumage, pale flesh-coloured legs.
- —*Stewart Island:* similar to South Island but with dark legs. (Largest of group)

Distribution and Habitat:
- —throughout New Zealand in native bush, second growth and scrubland.
- —least common in South Island and not seen west of main divide.
- —feeds on worms, insects, berries and seeds, most located by smell.

Breeding:
- —throughout year especially July to February.
- —Nest: in hollow logs, under tree roots, and in holes in banks.
- —Eggs: normally 1-2, smooth ivory or greenish-white.
- —male only incubates and cares for young.

Note:
The Little Spotted Kiwi *(Apteryx oweni)* and Great Spotted Kiwi *(Apteryx haasti)* are found in the South Island generally west of the main divide. Coloured grey, banded and mottled with brownish-black. These are respectively the smallest and largest of the Kiwis.

PLATE 1

13

YELLOW-EYED
PENGUIN

FIORDLAND CRESTED
PENGUIN

Yellow-eyed Penguin

(Hoiho)

Megadyptes antipodes
Family: SPHENISCIDAE

Endemic: (Fully protected).

Field Characters:
- largest of New Zealand mainland penguins.
- Adult: distinctive yellow eye and yellow band right round head.
- Immature: grey eye and no yellow band.

Distribution and Habitat:
- on coast from Banks Peninsula to Southland and Stewart Island, straggling to Cook Strait.
- feeds on small fish and squid.

Breeding:
- September to December.
- Nest: of sticks and coarse grass in scattered colonies throughout scrubland or coastal bush, sometimes up to 300 feet.
- Eggs: 2, white.

Fiordland Crested Penguin

Eudyptes pachyrhynchus,
Family: SPHENISCIDAE

Endemic: Three closely related sub-species. (Fully protected).

Field Characters:
- strongly hooked heavy bill.
- yellow stripe above eye extending backwards into separate crests.
- white bases to cheek feathers obvious when bird is excited.
- Immature: white throat, little or no crest.

Distribution and Habitat:
- South Westland, Fiordland and Stewart Island in coastal native bush.
- feeds on small fish, squid and krill.

Breeding:
- July to September.
- Nest: of sticks and leaves in scattered colonies among rocks, in caves and cavities beneath tree roots.
- Eggs: 1-2, white. *(continued on page 19)*

PLATE 2　　　　　　　　　　　　　　　　　　　　15

WHITE-FLIPPERED
PENGUIN

BLUE PENGUIN

Blue Penguin

(Korora)

Eudyptula minor
Female: SPHENISCIDAE

Native: Several closely related sub-species in New Zealand. Also occurs in Southern Australia from Perth to Sydney and Tasmania. (Fully protected).

Field Characters:
- —smallest of all penguins.
- —variable shades of blue on back, white below.
- —nocturnal on land and except when breeding spends day at sea.
- —males have heavier bills than females.
- —long wailing call of variable pitch.

Distribution and Habitat:
- —plentiful round New Zealand coasts.
- —feeds mainly on small fish and fish larvae.

Breeding:
- —August to November.
- —Nest: of grasses and sticks in caves, crevices, under boulders, in self-dug burrows under stumps, small bushes and flax up to 1,000 feet.
- —Sometimes under houses and in sheds.
- —Eggs: 1-2, white.

White-flippered Penguin

Eudyptula albosignata
Family: SPHENISCIDAE

Endemic: (Fully protected).

Field Characters:
- —larger and lighter in colour than Blue Penguin.
- —front edge of flipper white.
- —variable amount of white on tail and rump.

Distribution and Habitat:
- —generally Banks Peninsula and Canterbury coast where it is locally plentiful.
- —straggling to Cook Strait in North and Otago Peninsula in South.
- —habitat and food as for Blue Penguin.

(continued on page 19)

PLATE 3

17

AUSTRALASIAN GANNET

Adult

Juvenile

Australasian Gannet

(Takapu)

Sula bassana

Family: SULIDAE

Native: Also occurs Southern Australia. Two related sub-species in South Africa and North Atlantic. (Fully protected).

Field Characters:
- the size of a goose.
- Adult: white body contrasting with black trailing edge of wing. Yellow head not obvious at sea.
- Juvenile: white undersides, grey streaked head and neck, slate-grey back with white spots.
- often in flocks, diving from considerable height for food.

Distribution and Habitat:
- mainly round North Island in summer, dispersing widely in winter.
- breeding mainly on offshore islands round northern half of North Island.
- only mainland colony at Cape Kidnappers.
- most juveniles spend at least first two years in Australian waters.
- feeds by diving for small fish and squid.

Breeding:
- August to December.
- Nest: cup-shaped mound of seaweed, grasses and iceplant cemented with droppings, in closely packed colonies.
- Eggs: 1, pale bluish or greenish-white with chalky surface.

(continued from page 15)

Note:

Other crested Penguins breed on New Zealand sub-antarctic islands and straggle to mainland.

(continued from page 17)

Breeding:
- August to November.
- Nest and Eggs: similar to Blue Penguin.

PLATE 4

19

PIED SHAG

BLACK SHAG

Black Shag

Phalacrocorax carbo

(Kawau)

Family: PHALACROCORACIDAE

Native: Similar sub-species also in Australia, Europe, Africa, Asia and North America. (Not protected).

Field Characters:
- largest shag in New Zealand.
- white thigh patch, and greenish-black head plumes only in breeding season.
- Immature: browner than adult, and generally lighter on undersides.

Distribution and Habitat:
- throughout country on inland lakes, rivers, lagoons and sea coast.
- feeds by diving from surface for fish, freshwater crayfish and eels.
- there is little factual evidence to support reputed damage to trout fisheries.

Breeding:
- April to May and September to October, possibly 2 broods.
- Nest: large, of sticks, in colonies either on high trees or rock ledges, and on lower vantage points, close to, or surrounded by water.
- Eggs: 3-4, pale bluish-green with white chalky outer layer.

Pied Shag

Phalacrocorax varius

(Kahuriruhi)

Family: PHALACROCORACIDAE

Native: Similar sub-species also in Australia and Tasmania. (Fully protected).

Field Characters:
- slightly smaller than Black Shag.
- sides of face, neck, underparts white, thighs black.
- Immature: blackish-brown above, white below variably mottled with blackish-brown.

Distribution and Habitat:
- on coast throughout country, more numerous in north of both main islands, and Stewart Island, rarely inland.
- feeds mainly on marine fish, and occasionally in freshwater.

(continued on page 25)

PLATE 5

21

LITTLE SHAG

Immature

Adult

LITTLE BLACK
SHAG

Little Black Shag

Phalacrocorax sulcirostris

Family: PHALACROCORACIDAE

Native: Also Australia and South-west Pacific. (Fully protected).

Field Characters:
- slightly smaller than Little Shag.
- long slender *dark* bill and *short* tail.
- no crest at any stage.
- scalloped appearance of back and wing plumage.

Distribution and Habitat:
- North Island, more common in northern half, breeding in only a few localities.
- fresh-water lakes, salt-water lagoons and coast.
- feeds often in groups, by diving from surface, on small fish and eels.

Breeding:
- possibly February to May, September to December.
- Nest: of sticks and grasses in tree colonies, may be mixed with colonies of Little Shags, Black and Pied Shags.
- Eggs: 2-4, pale blue with white chalky outer layer.

Little Shag

(Kawaupaka)

Phalacrocorax melanoleucos

Family: PHALACROCORACIDAE

Native: Similar sub-species in Australia and South-west Pacific. (Fully protected).

Field Characters:
- small shag.
- short *yellow* bill, *long* tail.
- Adult: white cheeks and variable amount of white on undersides from white throat only to completely white below. Small black crest on forehead in breeding season.
- Immature: *All* black with *yellow* bill.

Distribution and Habitat:
- throughout country on fresh water, coastline, and into mountains.
- most common of freshwater shags.
- feeds by diving from surface on fish, eels, fresh water crayfish and aquatic insect larvae.

(continued on page 25)

PLATE 6

23

STEWART ISLAND SHAG

Bronze phase

Pied phase

Stewart Island *Leucocarbo carunculatus chalconotus*
Shag
Family: PHALACROCORACIDAE

Endemic: Two closely related sub-species in New Zealand. (Fully protected).

Field Characters:
- slightly smaller than Black Shag.
- two colour phases "*Bronze*" and "*Pied*" in approximately equal proportions.
- conspicuous white wing and back patches distinguish "Pied Phase" from Pied Shag in Plate 5.
- *pink* feet.
- large head prominent in flight.

Distribution and Habitat:
- from Otago Peninsula to Foveaux Strait and Stewart Island.
- only in coastal waters.
- feeds on small fish.

Breeding:
- July to September.
- Nest: cup-shaped of grasses and seaweed cemented with droppings, in tight colonies on cliffs and rocky islands.
- Eggs: 2-3, pale green with thin white chalky outer layer.
- both "phases" interbreed producing either "bronze" or "pied" young.

(continued from page 21)

Breeding:
- Similar to Black Shag, often in mixed colonies with Black Shags, and Little Shags.
- Eggs: 2-4, pale blue, covered with white chalky outer layer.

(continued from page 23)

Breeding:
- September to November.
- Nest: of sticks in colonies above or near water, often mixed with Pied and Black Shags.
- Eggs: 3-4, pale blue with white chalky outer layer.

PLATE 7   25

SPOTTED SHAG

Immature

Adult

Spotted Shag

(Parekareka)

Stictocarbo punctatus

Family: PHALACROCORACIDAE

Endemic: Also 2 closely related sub-species in New Zealand. (Fully protected).

Field Characters:
- large slender shag.
- generally dark grey above and light grey below with white stripe along side of head and neck.
- feet, variably pale whitish-yellow to chrome-yellow.
- Adult: shows ornamental crest and plumes *only* during early breeding season.
- Immature: all grey head and underparts.

Distribution and Habitat:
- common, but patchily distributed throughout North and South Island.
- only seen on coast.
- feeds on small fish and crustacea.

Breeding:
- Throughout year.
- Nest: of sticks, cliff plants and seaweed, in colonies on ledges, fissures in steep cliffs or sea caves preferably with overhead cover.
- Eggs: 2-4, pale blue with chalky outer layer.

Note:
Blue Shag *(Stictocarbo p. steadi)* generally found at Stewart Island, Foveaux Strait, and West Coast of South Island. Somewhat darker in plumage.

PLATE 8

27

WHITE HERON

ROYAL SPOONBILL

White Heron

Egretta alba

(Kotuku)

Family: ARDEIDAE

Native: Also Australia and closely related sub-species throughout world. (Fully protected).

Field Characters:
- larger than Reef Heron.
- pure white, *yellow* bill, black legs.
- adult bill black *only* during early breeding season.
- neck retracted in flight, slow leisurely wing beat.

Distribution and Habitat:
- in small numbers throughout country, breeding *only* at Okarito, South Westland.
- disperse outside breeding season generally to lake edges, ponds and marshes.
- feeds on small fish, frogs, insects and occasionally small birds with quick stabbing of bill.

Breeding:
- September to October.
- Nest: of twigs in colony on low trees and tree ferns near water.
- Eggs: 3-4, pale bluish-green.

Royal Spoonbill

Platalea regia

(Kotuku-ngutu-papa)

Family: THRESKIORNITHIDAE

Native: Self-introduced since 1850s, also in Australia and New Guinea. (Fully protected).

Field Characters:
- slightly bigger than White Heron.
- face, large flattened bill and legs black.
- neck *extended* in flight.
- Immature; varying amount of black on flight feathers visible when flying.

Distribution and Habitat:
- less common than White Heron, throughout country, only breeding at Okarito associated with White Herons.
- disperses to river estuaries and lagoons outside breeding season.

(continued on page 31)

PLATE 9

29

REEF HERON

Reef Heron

(Matuku-moana)

Egretta sacra

Family: ARDEIDAE

Native: Also Asia, Australia and Southwest Pacific. (Fully protected). **Note:** A white form occurs throughout northern part of range outside New Zealand.

Field Characters:
- similar to, but *much darker* than White-faced Heron.
- dark slate-blue all over.
- neck retracted in flight, slow leisurely wing beat.
- normally singly or in pairs.

Distribution and Habitat:
- throughout country only on sheltered rocky coastline, becoming more sparingly distributed.
- commonest in northern half of North Island and larger offshore islands, frequenting mudflats and intertidal zone.
- feeds close inshore on small fish and crabs.

Breeding:
- September to February.
- Nest: of sticks, well hidden in shallow caves or crevices, or among bushes on steep cliffs, not far from water.
- Eggs: usually 3, pale greenish-blue.

(continued from page 29)

- feeds on small crustacea in *shallow* water by sidesweeping tip of bill through water.

Breeding:
- November to December.
- Nest: of sticks, in colony, on higher trees than White Heron.
- Eggs: 3-4, white, sparingly marked with brown blotches.

PLATE 10 31

BLUE DUCK

Blue Duck

(Whio)

Hymenolaimus malacoryhynchos

Family: ANATIDAE

Endemic: (Fully protected).

Field Characters:
—smaller than Mallard.
—dove grey, heavily spotted with chestnut on breast.
—prominent narrow bill, pinkish-white with black edge to tip.
—Immature: similar, but no chestnut spotting on breast.
—Male has characteristic whistling call; female a gutteral rattle.
—singly, in pairs or family groups.

Distribution and Habitat:
—North and South Islands now restricted to mountain and bush streams in undeveloped areas.
—feeds by diving mainly on insect larvae.

Breeding:
—August to November.
—Nest: lined with down, on ground under thick vegetation or in holes, close to or above a stream.
—Eggs: 4-9, creamy-white.

PLATE 11

33

NEW ZEALAND
FALCON

Adult
♀

Immature
♂

New Zealand Falcon

Falco novaeseelandiae

(Karearea)

Family: FALCONIDAE

Endemic: (Fully protected).

Field Characters:
- about half size of Australasian Harrier.
- Females generally much larger than males.
- Adult: upper parts appearing black, but feathers striped with buff.
- underparts light cream with dark streaks, thighs rusty red.
- feet and naked skin at base of bill, yellow.
- Immature: dark blackish-brown above and all dark chocolate-brown below.
- feet and naked skin at base of bill, lead-grey.
- call a piercing whistle or scream, "Kek kek kek".

Distribution and Habitat:
- distributed generally throughout New Zealand in native bush and isolated high back-country valleys.
- feeds mainly on birds up to duck size and occasionally small mammals, e.g. mice.

Breeding:
- October to November.
- Nest: of grass or sticks under overhanging rocks on steep slopes or in high trees.
- Eggs: 2-4, rich reddish-brown with darker blotches.
- Female only incubates.

PLATE 12

35

WEKA

Western

North Island

Weka

Family: RALLIDAE

Endemic: Four closely related sub-species, North Island and Western Weka shown in plate. (Fully protected except on Chatham Islands).

Field Characters:
- inquisitive, flightless, measured walk, flicking tail, rapid run.
- *North Island:* smallest, with grey undersides and brown legs.
- *Western:* generally larger than North Island and with two colour phases, "Brown" phase similar to North Island, but with pink feet and less grey on underside. "Black" phase blackish-brown all over with red-brown feet.
- *Buff:* very similar to Western with red-brown legs and feet, also lighter (buff) plumage.
- *Stewart Island:* similar but smaller than Western with no dark streaking on flanks.

Distribution and Habitat:
- In North Island, restricted to Gisborne, Poverty Bay, but have recently been reintroduced elsewhere
- In South Island, Western Weka are locally common from Nelson-Marlborough to Fiordland generally west of main divide.
- Buff Weka previously on Canterbury Plains but restricted now to Chatham Islands (Introduced).
- Stewart Island Weka now present on Stewart Island and various southern islands where they were introduced by fishermen, whalers, sealers and mutton-birders.
- feeds on a wide variety of animal and vegetable matter, insects, crustacea, worms, fruits, rats and mice, eggs and chicks of ground-nesting birds.

Breeding:
- commonly September to April, but sometimes 3-4 times a year.
- Nest: shallow cup of woven grass under scrub, tussock, raupo according to locality.
- Eggs: 3-6, creamy-pink with scattered mauve blotches.

PLATE 13   37

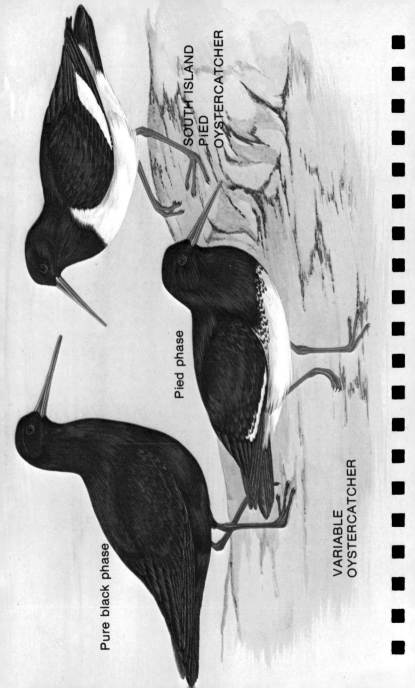

SOUTH ISLAND PIED OYSTERCATCHER

Pied phase

Pure black phase

VARIABLE OYSTERCATCHER

South Island Pied Oystercatcher (Torea)

Haematopus ostralegus
Family: HAEMATOPODIDAE

Native: Similar sub-species also in Australia, South America and Northern Hemisphere. (Fully protected).

Field Characters:
- conspicuous, black upper parts sharply separated from white below.
- white of breast extending above and in front of closed wing.
- in flight, prominent broad white wing stripe and white back from rump to shoulders.

Distribution and Habitat:
- breeds inland on South Island riverbeds.
- from January to August found on coast throughout New Zealand in large flocks mainly on estuaries, mudflats and paddocks.
- feeds on crustacea, shellfish, worms and larvae.

Breeding:
- September to November.
- Nest: Scrape mainly in river sand or shingle.
- Eggs: 2-3, variable from pale brown to cream with dark brown and black spots and blotches all over.

Variable Oystercatcher

Haematopus unicolor
Family: HAEMATOPODIDAE

Endemic: (Fully protected).

Field Characters:
- larger than South Island Pied Oystercatcher.
- 2 basic colour phases: *"Pure Black"*, and *"Pied"*. The latter differs from South Island Pied by smudgy separation between black and white on underside and *no white on shoulder in front of wing.*

- narrow white wing stripe, and white only on *lower* back.
- many birds show intermediate plumages between both above phases and pairs may consist of both phases.

Distribution and Habitat:
- Only on beaches and coast throughout New Zealand and many offshore islands.

(continued on page 41)

PLATE 14　　　　　　　　　　　　　　　　　　　39

BANDED DOTTEREL

♂

♀

Immature

Banded Dotterel

(Tuturiwhatu)

Charadrius bicinctus
Family: CHARADRIIDAE

Endemic: (Fully protected).

Field Characters:
- size similar to Song Thrush.
- dumpy bird with very short tail.
- Female: colours of bands less intense and *no* black forehead above white stripe.
- Immature and Winter Adult: bands on breast and black stripe on face *absent*.
- short rushing runs, bobbing movements when stopped.
- high pitched staccato "pit pit" call.

Distribution and Habitat:
- throughout New Zealand on coasts, riverbeds and lake shores.
- following breeding, inland birds move to coast, while there is a general northward movement and concentration in northern New Zealand in winter.
- some, probably immature birds, move across Tasman to winter in Australia.

Breeding:
- August to December.
- Nest: scrape in sand or shingle rarely with nesting material.
- Eggs: normally 3, greyish or greenish closely marked with dark brown or black spots and blotches all over.

(continued from page 39)

- feeds on shellfish, crustacea and worms.

Breeding:
- October to January.
- Nest: scrape in beach sand or shingle.
- Eggs: 2-3, stone-buff spotted and blotched with dark brown.

PLATE 15   41

BLACK-FRONTED DOTTEREL

Black-fronted Dotterel

Charadrius melanops
Family: CHARADRIIDAE

Native: Australia, self-introduced 1950s. (Fully protected).

Field Characters:
- smaller than Banded Dotterel.
- striking black and white design on head.
- broad black *V*-shaped band on breast, not present in Immature.
- chestnut-brown patch on shoulder.
- voice is high-pitched whistle or soft "Tink Tink".

Distribution and Habitat:
- first seen Hawke's Bay and now common in Central Hawke's Bay, shingle riverbeds, spreading to Wairarapa, Manawatu and east coast of South Island.
- in New Zealand breeding on riverbeds generally not far inland, but in Australia is mainly inland on edges of stagnant water.
- feeds on aquatic insects and invertebrates.

Breeding:
- September to January.
- Nest: generally a scrape among grass and shingle, sometimes in open.
- Eggs: normally 3, yellowish-stone heavily spotted and marked all over with dark brown.

PLATE 16

43

WRYBILL

Breeding

Non-breeding

Wrybill

(Ngutu parore)

Anarhynchus frontalis
Family: CHARADRIIDAE

Endemic: (Fully protected).

Field Characters:
- —somewhat smaller than Banded Dotterel.
- —uniform light grey above.
- —pure white below with black "collar" in breeding plumage only.
- —bill black, long, pointed, and tip bent to right side.

Distribution and Habitat:
- —breeds on South Island broad shingle riverbeds east of main divide in Canterbury and North Otago.
- —from December to July on mudflats and estuaries, the majority migrating to the Auckland area but smaller numbers may be found elsewhere.
- —feeds on insects and small invertebrates.

Breeding:
- —September to November.
- —Nest: small scrape in river sand or shingle.
- —Eggs: normally 2, light grey evenly covered with minute dark spots.

PLATE 17

45

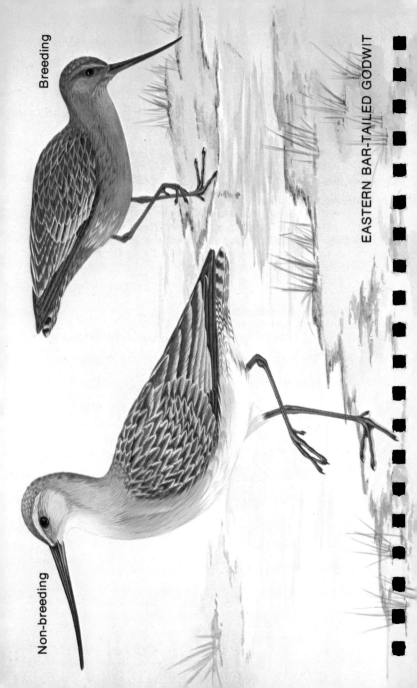

Breeding

Non-breeding

EASTERN BAR-TAILED GODWIT

Eastern Bar-tailed Godwit   *Limosa lapponica*

(Kuaka)   Family: SCOLOPACIDAE

Migrant: From North-east Siberia and Alaska. Closely related sub-species in North Europe. (Fully protected).

Field Characters:
   —body smaller than Oystercatcher.
   —long black slender legs.
   —long slightly upturned bill.
   —"Non-Breeding" plumage generally mottled greyish-buff from September to February.
   —"Breeding" plumage starting to appear in February except for Immature which retain non-breeding plumage throughout first year.

Distribution and Habitat:
   —arrive in New Zealand in September and majority depart in late March. Some non-breeding birds remain here during our winter.
   —found mainly in flocks on coastal marshes and mudflats throughout New Zealand with concentrations in Auckland, Farewell Spit, Christchurch and Invercargill.
   —feeds on small marine invertebrates, crustacea and molluscs.

Breeding:
   —May to June.
   —Nesting in North-east Siberia and Alaska.
   —Eggs: normally 4, large greenish-brown with dark brown blotches.

PLATE 18   47

PIED STILT

Pied Stilt

Himantopus himantopus

(Poaka)

Family: RECURVIROSTRIDAE

Native: Throughout world in temperate and tropical regions.
(Fully protected).

Field Characters:
- striking black and white plumage.
- long spindly pink legs, trailing far beyond tail in flight.
- long straight awl-like bill.
- monotonous yapping call.
- Immature: back of neck *grey* and often with dark smudges round eye.

Distribution and Habitat:
- common throughout New Zealand anywhere there is water up to 3000 feet.
- on lake edges, marshes, wet paddocks and riverbeds, moving from inland areas to coast in autumn.
- feeds on aquatic insects, worms, snails and shellfish.

Breeding:
- September to January.
- Nest: from scrapes in shingle, lined with a little grass to substantial nests with variable amounts of grass and weeds, on ground close to or surrounded by shallow water.
- Mostly in open but sometimes in clumps of grass.
- Eggs: normally 4, from buff to olive-brown heavily marked all over with black and brown spots and blotches.

Note:

The closely related Black Stilt *(Himantopus novaezealandiae)* is relatively rare, breeding only within the Waitaki River system in South Canterbury.

PLATE 19

49

SOUTHERN BLACK-BACKED GULL

Adult

Second year

First year

Southern Black-backed Gull (Karoro)

Larus dominicanus
Family: LARIDAE

Native: Circumpolar in southern temperate to sub-antarctic regions.
(Not protected).

Field Characters:
- largest of 3 New Zealand gulls.
- Adult: black and white, with white tips to flight feathers and *pure white tail*.
- First Year: mottled greyish-brown with *dark* bill.
- Second Year: very variable, ranging from close to first year to adult with no white tips to flight feathers and some *black* in tail.

Distribution and Habitat:
- throughout New Zealand on or near coast.
- wanders far inland to farmland and even alpine regions.
- feeds on any accessible animal food, often entirely by scavenging.
- commonly seen in large flocks frequenting dumps, riverbeds and fields.

Breeding:
- October to December.
- Nest: fairly bulky collection of grasses and other plants often pulled up by roots.
- May be singly or in large colonies.
- Eggs: normally 3, variable from light blue to dark olive-brown with brown and black spots and blotches.

PLATE 20

51

RED-BILLED GULL

Adult

Immature

Red-billed Gull

Larus novaehollandiae

(Tarapunga)

Family: LARIDAE

Native: Also Australia and South Africa. (Fully protected).

Field Characters:
- half size of Black-backed Gull.
- white body, pearly grey back, black wing feathers tipped with white.
- Adult: short red bill, bright red legs, feet and eye ring.
- Immature: dark brown to brownish-red bill, purplish brown legs and feet, brown spots on back and wing coverts (these spots not generally present after July of first winter).

Distribution and Habitat:
- throughout New Zealand especially on coasts and offshore islands, occasionally inland.
- often in large flocks.
- feeds on small fish, crustacea, worms, sometimes berries, and also scavenging on dead animal matter.

Breeding:
- October to December.
- Nest: of seaweed, grasses and ice plant, in tight colonies from a few to thousands of birds, on islands, rocky headlands, cliffs and beaches.
- Eggs: 2-3, colour variable grey to brown with light and dark brown blotches all over.

PLATE 21

53

BLACK-BILLED GULL

Immature

Black-billed Gull

(Tarapunga)

Larus bulleri

Family: LARIDAE

Endemic: (Fully protected).

Field Characters:
- — similar in size to Red-billed Gull.
- — in flight the mainly white outer flight feathers distinguish it from the Red-billed Gull who has mainly black flight feathers.
- — Adult: bill, *black*, more slender and longer than Red-billed Gull, legs and feet reddish-black.
- — Immature: similar to immature Red-billed Gull but having longer bill which is pinkish or orange with black tip.

Distribution and Habitat:
- — breeding mainly in South Island on larger shingle riverbeds.
- — Uncommon in North Island, but regular colonies at Rotorua, Hawke's Bay, and Poverty Bay.
- — following breeding season inland birds move to coast and there is also a northward movement across Cook Strait.
- — feeds on aquatic and land insects, often seen in freshly ploughed fields, also scavenging in towns during winter.

Breeding:
- — October to December.
- — Nest: of grasses and other plant matter in tight colonies.
- — Eggs: 2-3, similar to Red-billed Gull, but generally lighter in colour.

PLATE 22

55

BLACK-FRONTED TERN

Black-fronted Tern

(Tara)

Chlidonias hybrida

Family: STERNIDAE

Native: Similar sub-species in Australia, Europe, South Asia and
Africa. (Fully protected).

Field Characters:
—small grey tern, with black cap and white stripe under eye.
—bill and feet bright orange.
—white rump noticeable in flight.
—Immature: head speckled brown, darkest on nape, bill dark
brown.
—call a high-pitched staccato whistling at intervals, with harsh
"yark" near breeding colony.

Distribution and Habitat:
—only breeding South Island, inland on shingle riverbeds east
of main ranges.
—during the winter move to coast, also to North Island in small
numbers.
—feeds on small fish, water insects and larvae, may "hawk"
for caterpillars, flying insects and moths. Commonly seen
following plough or harrows during cultivation of fields.

Breeding:
—October to January.
—Nest: scrape in sand or shingle in loose colonies sometimes
associated with Black-billed Gulls.
—Eggs: 1-3, variable from dark stone to live-brown with large
light or dark brown blotches all over.

PLATE 23

57

CASPIAN TERN

Caspian Tern

(Taranui)

Hydroprogne caspia
Family: STERNIDAE

Native: Throughout world in tropical and temperate zone. (Fully protected).

Field Characters:
- very large tern, bigger than Red-billed Gull.
- light grey above, white below.
- black cap and feet, large red bill.
- Immature: with mottled cap similar to adult outside breeding season.
- over water, downward pointing head in flight.
- voice is a raucous drawn-out "kaah".

Distribution and Habitat:
- North and South Island, more plentiful in north.
- generally singly or in pairs frequenting coastal estuaries and penetrating inland along rivers.
- feeds on small fish by plunge diving.

Breeding:
- September to January.
- Nest: scrape in sand or shingle mainly in colonies on shingle banks, sandy beaches and dunes.
- isolated nests on rocky promontories.
- occasionally inland near fresh-water lakes.
- Eggs: 1-3, light stone with dark brown spots and blotches.

PLATE 24

59

WHITE-FRONTED TERN

White-fronted Tern

Sterna striata

(Tara)

Family: STERNIDAE

Endemic: (Fully protected).

Field Characters:
- size between Caspian and Black-fronted Terns.
- silver grey above, white below, bill and feet black.
- large black cap and white stripe (much extended in winter) on forehead.
- deeply forked light grey tail.
- Juvenile: cap lightly mottled with brown or buff, back and wings barred with black stripes.

Distribution and Habitat:
- throughout New Zealand mainly on coast.
- many juveniles cross Tasman and spend at least their first winter on the east Australian coast.
- feeds mainly on shoaling small fish by plunge diving from the air.

Breeding:
- October to January.
- Nest: on bare rock or scrape in sand or shingle, but sometimes of variable amounts of grasses, twigs and ice-plant.
- in colonies of a few to several hundred often associated with Red-billed Gulls.
- Eggs: 1-2, variable light stone, green or brown with small scattered light and dark brown blotches.

PLATE 25

61

NEW ZEALAND PIGEON

New Zealand Pigeon *Hemiphaga novaeseelandiae*

(Kereru)

Family: COLUMBIDAE

Endemic: One closely related sub-species in the Chatham
Islands. (Fully protected).

Field Characters:
- large, distinctively coloured irridescent green with coppery
   reflections, white underparts.
- heavy flight with loud swishing of wings.
- spectacular rising and falling nuptual flights in spring.

Distribution and Habitat:
- throughout New Zealand, now mainly restricted to native
   bush. Unfortunately in some districts poaching still occurs.
- feeds on young leaves, the flowers and fruits of native trees.
- has adapted to introduced plants and feeds on tree lucerne,
   clover, willows and plums etc.

Breeding:
- mainly November to January.
- Nest: flimsy structure of twigs in trees and shrubs.
- Eggs: 1, pure white.

PLATE 26

KEA

SOUTH ISLAND KAKA

Kaka

Nestor meridionalis
Family: NESTORIDAE

Endemic: Two closely related sub-species, one in North Island and one in Southern Islands. (Fully protected).

Field Characters:
- somewhat smaller than New Zealand Pigeon.
- large hooked bill.
- light crown and nape, bright scarlet underwing.
- North Island sub-species, greyer on crown, less red on belly, more chocolate-brown then green in general colour.
- voice a raucous "ka-aa" and melodious whistle.

Distribution and Habitat:
- mainly confined to larger areas of native bush and some off-shore island sanctuaries, e.g. Kapiti and Little Barrier Island.
- rarely into exotic plantations and gardens.
- feeds on nectar, berries, grubs and seeds.

Breeding:
- November to January.
- Nest: in hollow trees without nest material.
- Eggs: 4-5, white.

Kea

Nestor notabilis
Family: NESTORIDAE

Endemic: (Partially protected).

Field Characters:
- size similar to Kaka.
- mainly olive-green with orange-red on rump and under wing.
- harsh "kee-a" call mainly in flight.

Distribution and Habitat:
- generally only in South Island high country from Marlborough-Nelson to Fiordland, but reaching coast during winter in Nelson and Westland.
- most commonly seen above bushline, but also present in native bush.
- feeds on roots, leaves, buds, fruits. insects and nectar.

(continued on page 67)

PLATE 27   65

EASTERN ROSELLA

Eastern Rosella

Platycercus eximius
Family: PLATYCERCIDAE

Introduced: From cage-escaped birds. Also found in Eastern Australia. (Not protected).

Field Characters:
- —twice size of Parakeet.
- —strikingly and brilliantly coloured.
- —very rapid wing beat in flight.
- —prominent long tail.

Distribution and Habitat:
- —common in native bush north of the Waikato, also western Wairarapa, Upper Hutt valley and Dunedin.
- —feeds on berries, seeds, flowers, and occasionally fruit.

Breeding:
- —nests in holes in hollow branches or trees. Further details unknown in New Zealand.
- —In Australia breeds from August to January.
- —Eggs: 4-7, white.
- —Female only incubates.

(continued from page 65)

Breeding:
- —August to December.
- —Nest: on ground in crevices or holes in logs, occasionally with twigs and leaves for nesting material.
- —Eggs: 2-4, white.

PLATE 28 67

RED-CROWNED PARAKEET

YELLOW-
CROWNED PARAKEET

Red-crowned Parakeet (Kakariki)

Cyanoramphus novaezelandiae

Family: PLATYCERCIDAE

Native: Also New Caledonia. Several closely related sub-species in New Zealand region. (Fully protected).

Field Characters:
- small parrot, size of Blackbird.
- red forehead and crown.
- red patch *behind* eye.
- rapid wing beat, swift straight flight.
- chattering call mainly when in flight.

Distribution and Habitat:
- some large areas of native bush on mainland more plentiful on outlying islands.
- feeds on wide variety of vegetable matter from fruits and seeds to leaves and buds.
- commonly held in aviaries under permit.

Breeding:
- October to March.
- Nest: deposits eggs in hollow trees and rock crevices.
- Eggs: 4-9, white.
- Female only incubates.

Yellow-crowned Parakeet (Kakariki)

Cyanoramphus auriceps

Family: PLATYCERCIDAE

Endemic: One other closely related sub-species. (Fully protected).

Field Characters:
- smaller than Red-crowned Parakeet.
- red forehead, *yellow* crown.
- no red behind eye.
- flight and call similar to Red-crowned Parakeet.

Distribution and Habitat:
- similar to Red-crowned Parakeet, but more plentiful and widespread on the mainland.
- food similar to Red-crowned Parakeet.
- commonly held in aviaries under permit.

(continued on page 73)

PLATE 29

69

LONG-TAILED CUCKOO

SHINING CUCKOO

Shining Cuckoo

(Pupiwharauroa)

Chalcites lucidus
Family: CUCULIDAE

Native (Migratory): Only breeding in New Zealand. (Fully protected).

Field Characters:
- size of House Sparrow.
- more often heard than seen.
- Female and Immature: duller and with less distinct bars on cheeks.
- voice, a musical series of double notes with downward slur at end of call.

Distribution and Habitat:
- throughout New Zealand up to 4,000 feet.
- arriving in August, migrating north in February to Solomon Islands and Bismark Archipelago.
- feeds on insects and caterpillars.

Breeding:
- October to January.
- lays eggs in nest of mainly Grey Warbler, but also Fantail, Tit, and Silvereye.
- Eggs: 1 per nest of host, total number per season unknown, greenish or bluish-white to olive-brown.
- when chick hatches eggs or chicks of host are ejected by foster chick.

Long-tailed Cuckoo

(Koekoea)

Eudynamis taitensis
Family: CUCULIDAE

Native (Migratory): Only breeding in New Zealand. (Fully protected).

Field Characters:
- bigger than Blackbird, tail longer than body.
- Immature: differ by being greyish-brown speckled all over above with pale spots, undersides reddish-buff with fine dark streaks.
- voice, long harsh piercing screech.

(continued on page 73)

PLATE 30

71

MOREPORK

Morepork

(Ruru)   Family: STRIGIDAE

Native: Also Australia and New Guinea. (Fully protected).

Field Characters:
- —generally nocturnal and usually heard rather than seen.
- —voice, clear almost "quor-coo" with falling second syllable. Also harsh and vibrating screech.

Distribution and Habitat:
- —throughout New Zealand in native and introduced forest, also close to settlement in parks and gardens.
- —often seen at late dusk on prominent perch or hawking for food.
- —feeds mainly on moths and insects including Wetas, also lizards, mice, rats, and small birds.

Breeding:
- —October to November.
- —Nest: generally in hollow trees, but also in dense clumps of vegetation, rarely in open.
- —Eggs: 2-3, white.
- —Female only incubates and broods chicks.

(continued from page 69)

Breeding:
- —August to April.
- —Nest and Eggs: as for Red-crowned Parakeet.
- —Female only incubates.

(continued from page 71)

Distribution and Habitat:
- —throughout New Zealand arriving in September to October, migrating north in February to South-west Pacific Islands.
- —feeds on insects, lizards, young birds and eggs.

Breeding:
- —November to December.
- —lays egg in nest of mainly Whitehead and Brown Creeper, but also Yellowhead, Tit, Robin, Silvereye.
- —Eggs: 1 per nest of host, total number per season unknown, creamy-white spotted and blotched all over with purplish-brown and grey.
- —Eggs and chicks of host ejected as with Shining Cuckoo.

PLATE 31   73

RIFLEMAN

♂

♀

Rifleman

(Titipounamu)

Acanthisitta chloris
Family: XENICIDAE

Endemic: Two closely related sub-species one in North Island and one in southern islands. (Fully protected).

Field Characters:
- smallest of New Zealand birds.
- Male: mainly green above.
- Female: streaked buff and dark brown above.
- tail black, tipped with buff and very short.
- continuously on move with vigorous wing flicking when on branches and tree trunks.
- voice, irregular very high pitched "zipt — zipt — zipt".

Distribution and Habitat:
- throughout New Zealand except north of Te Aroha, but also Great and Little Barrier Islands.
- in native and exotic forest up to bushline.
- feeds mainly on insects, small larvae and moths high in trees by searching among bark and foliage.

Breeding:
- August to January, generally 2 broods.
- Nest: closely woven of fine roots and leaves lined with feathers in hollow limbs, bark crevices and clay banks.
- Eggs: 2-4, white.

PLATE 32

75

ROCK WREN

Rock Wren

Xenicus gilviventris
Family: XENICIDAE

Endemic: (Fully protected).

Field Characters:
- between Silvereye and House Sparrow in size.
- very short tail, disproportionately large feet.
- rarely flies more than a few yards.
- frequent vigorous bobbing of body.
- often heard underfoot in rock piles.

Distribution and Habitat:
- only in South Island from Nelson to Fiordland.
- alpine and sub-alpine generally above scrubline, on or in rock falls and crevices.
- feeds actively on and under ground mainly on insects and spiders.

Breeding:
- September to November.
- Nest: in rock crevices or holes between rocks, a bulky igloo-shaped structure woven from snow tussock and may be generously lined with feathers.
- Eggs: 2-5, white.

PLATE 33

77

BROWN CREEPER

Brown Creeper

(Pipipi)

Finschia novaeseelandiae

Family: MUSCICAPIDAE

Endemic: (Fully protected).

Field Characters:
- —smaller than House Sparrow.
- —generally brown above and light buff below.
- —feeds in noisy flocks.

Distribution and Habitat:
- —only South Island, Stewart Island and their offlying islands.
- —mostly in native bush, but also in exotic plantations and scrub.
- —not in open country.
- —up to but not including sub-alpine.
- —feeds on insects, moths and grubs.

Breeding:
- —November to January.
- —Nest: neat cup woven of grass fibres and moss, lined with feathers, well hidden in tops of shrubs.
- —Eggs: 3-4, white, heavily blotched with brown and purplish-brown more dense at large end.
- —Female only incubates.
- —often a host to Long-tailed Cuckoo.

PLATE 34

79

WHITEHEAD

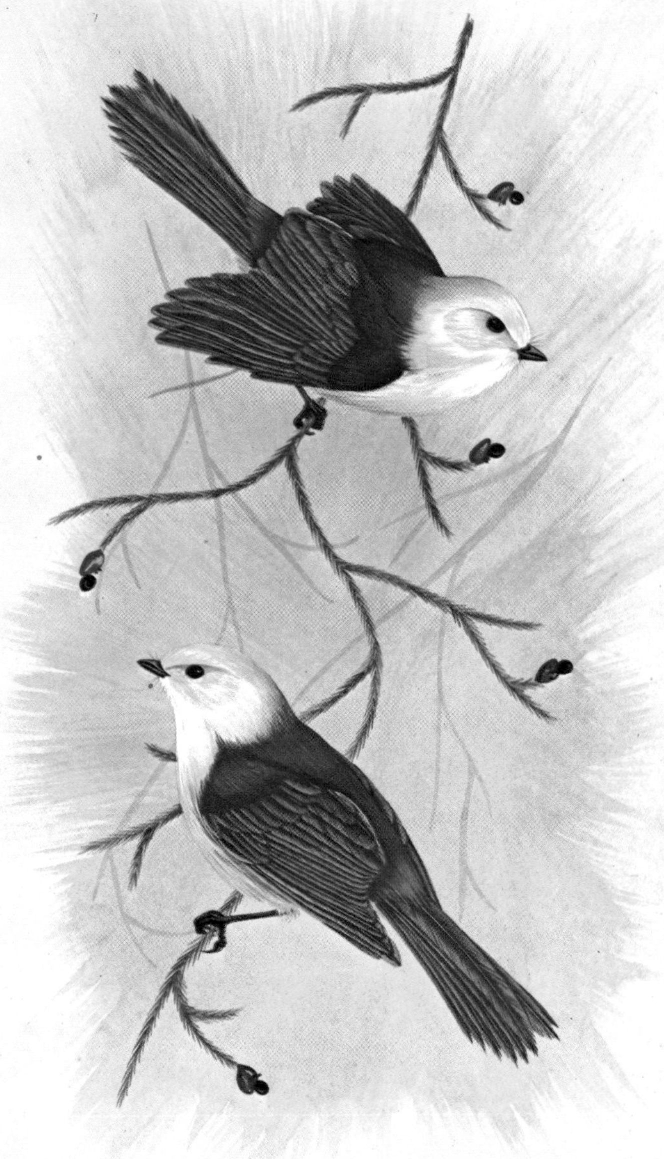

Whitehead

(Popokatea)

Mohoua albicilla

Family: MUSCICAPIDAE

Endemic: (Fully protected).

Field Characters:
- — size similar to Silvereye.
- — dull brown above, head and underparts white slightly tinged with brown, female duller on head.
- — except for breeding season is seen in noisy flocks.
- — voice, hard single "zit".

Distribution and Habitat:
- — North Island and associated large offshore islands.
- — locally plentiful from Te Aroha, Pirongia and East Cape southwards.
- — in native bush and major exotic forests.
- — feeds on insects in forest canopy, tree trunks and logs, also seeds and small soft fruits.

Breeding:
- — October to February.
- — Nest: bulky cup shaped nest of twigs, rootlets, grass and bark bound with spiders' web, lined with bark in canopy of shrubs or low trees.
- — Eggs: 2-4, translucent white, variably spotted with brown or reddish-brown.
- — often host to Long-tailed Cuckoo.

PLATE 35 81

YELLOWHEAD

Yellowhead

(Mohua)

Mohoua ochrocephala
Family: MUSCICAPIDAE

Endemic: (Fully protected).

Field Characters:
- size of House Sparrow.
- olive-green above with canary yellow head and chest.
- Female and Immature: have less yellow on nape.
- except for breeding season seen in flocks or family groups.
- voice, a musical canary-like call and a high pitched buzzing.

Distribution and Habitat:
- locally common in South Island beech forest.
- frequent dense native forest canopy and does not move into scrub areas like Brown Creeper.
- feeds on insects in foliage and in debris collected in tree forks and bark, occasionally on ground.

Breeding:
- November to December.
- Nest: cup-shaped of moss, rootlets and spiders' web lined with fine grass in natural holes in dead trees.
- Eggs: 3-4, pinkish-white, evenly blotched with reddish-brown.
- Female only incubates.
- sometimes host to Long-tailed Cuckoo.

PLATE 36

83

TIT

Yellow-breasted ♂

♀

Pied ♂

Tit

(Miro miro, Ngiru ngiru)

Petroica macrocephala
Family: MUSCICAPIDAE

Endemic: Five closely related sub-species with Pied and Yellow-breasted Tit illustrated in plate. (Fully protected).

Field Characters:
— size between House Sparrow and Silvereye.
— Female: as shown, for both sub-species, but may have slightly yellower undersides in Yellow-breasted Tit.
— Male *Pied:* black and white.
— Male *Yellow-breasted:* yellow undersides varying from pale yellow to orange-yellow with bright orange stripe at chest margin of black and yellow.
— both sexes have prominent white patch on wing, especially seen when in flight.
— song is a cheerful often repeated trill.

Distribution and Habitat:
— throughout New Zealand, with Pied in North Island, Yellow-breasted in South Island.
— in native and exotic forest.
— feeds on grubs and insects often caught in flight.

Breeding:
— September to February, 2 broods.
— Nest: of moss, bark and cobwebs lined with feathers, located in hollow in tree trunk, rock crevice or sometimes in branch fork up to 30 feet.
— Eggs: 3-4, cream, light yellowish and purplish-brown spots densest at larger end.
— Female only incubates.

PLATE 37
85

ROBIN

North Island

♂

South Island

♂

♀

Robin

(Toutouwai)

Petroica australis
Family: MUSCICAPIDAE

Endemic: Three closely related sub-species with North and South Island illustrated. (Fully protected).

Field Characters:
- smaller than Starling, bigger than House Sparrow.
- *North Island:*
- Male: *sooty-black,* with white streaks on head and throat, white belly and undertail.
- Female: slightly browner above with light cream belly and undertail.
- *South Island:*
- Male: *dusky-black,* lower breast, belly and undertail cream-buff.
- Female: slightly browner above.
- strikingly long legs.
- very tame and inquisitive.

Distribution and Habitat:
- throughout New Zealand, but localised in some areas.
- in both native and exotic forest.
- feeds on insects and small worms in lower levels of forest and on ground.

Breeding:
- August to February.
- Nest: rather bulky, of moss, bark, and roots bound with spiders' web lined with tree fern scales and soft grasses.
- in tree hollows, rock crevices and tree forks relatively lower than Tit.
- Eggs: 2-4, cream, with purplish-brown spots denser at larger end.
- Female only incubates.

PLATE 38

87

BELLBIRD ♂

♀

Bellbird

(Korimako, Makomako)

Anthornis melanura

Family: MELIPHAGIDAE

Endemic: One closely related sub-species. (Fully protected).

Field Characters:
- size between Song Thrush and House Sparrow.
- tail long with notched end.
- Male: purple gloss on head and face.
- Female: duller, with narrow white stripe on cheek.
- voice often confused with Tui, a liquid flute-like note and a sharp alarm call.

Distribution and Habitat:
- throughout New Zealand, but rarely seen north of Auckland on mainland.
- in forest, scrub, gardens and orchards.
- feeds on nectar, insects and fruit.
- pollen becomes attached to head when searching for nectar in flax and pohutukawa.

Breeding:
- September to January.
- Nest: loosely constructed of twigs and fibres with a deep cup well lined with feathers and fine grass.
- usually in dense cover up to 40 feet.
- Eggs: 3-4, pinkish-white, with reddish-brown spots and blotches densest at larger end.
- Female only incubates.

PLATE 39

89

TUI

Tui

Prosthemadera novaeseelandiae
Family: MELIPHAGIDAE

Endemic: One closely related sub-species. (Fully protected).

Field Characters:
- slightly bigger than Blackbird, male larger.
- prominent white tuft at throat and white patch on wing.
- middle of back dark brown, otherwise black with variable metallic sheen.
- loud whirring of wings especially when taking flight.
- voice similar to Bellbird but more resonant and having harsh croaks and gurgles especially at end of call.

Distribution and Habitat:
- throughout New Zealand up to 3,500 feet.
- primarily in native forest remnants, also gardens to which it is attracted by flowering trees and shrubs, rare in pure beech forest.
- feeds on nectar, fruits, berries and insects.
- forehead often pollen-stained.

Breeding:
- October to January, possibly 2 broods.
- Nest: bulky structure of sticks and twigs, cup lined with fine grasses, moss and feathers.
- Eggs: 3-4, pinkish-white with reddish-brown spots and blotches densest at larger end.
- Female only incubates.

PLATE 40

91

Index of Common Names
Volume 1 — Town, Pasture and Freshwater
Volume 2 — Mountain, Bush and Shore

Mallard	1	7
Morepork	2	31
Myna	1	37
Owl, Little	1	19
Oystercatcher, South Island Pied	2	14
Oystercatcher, Variable	2	14
Parakeet, Red-crowned	2	29
Parakeet, Yellow-crowned	2	29
Penguin, Blue	2	3
Penguin, Fiordland Crested	2	2
Penguin, White-flippered	2	3
Penguin, Yellow-eyed	2	2
Pheasant	1	13
Pigeon, New Zealand	2	26
Pigeon, Rock	1	18
Pipit	1	21
Plover, Spur-winged	1	17
Pukeko	1	15
Quail, Californian	1	12
Rail, Banded	1	14
Redpoll	1	34
Rifleman	2	32
Robin	2	38
Rook	1	40
Rosella, Eastern	2	28
Scaup	1	9
Shag, Black	2	5
Shag, Little	2	6
Shag, Little Black	2	6
Shag, Pied	2	5
Shag, Spotted	2	8
Shag, Stewart Island	2	7
Shoveler	1	10
Silvereye	1	29
Skylark	1	21
Sparrow, Hedge	1	23
Sparrow, House	1	35
Spoonbill, Royal	2	9
Starling	1	36
Stilt, Pied	2	19
Swallow, Welcome	1	22

ACKNOWLEDGEMENTS

The artist and the authors wish to acknowledge the assistance and advice of G. Marshall, the Dominion Museum and the staff of the Wildlife Branch, Department of Internal Affairs.

OTHER REED BOOKS

Birds in New Zealand

(Ed) C.J.R. Robertson

The second volume in the **Reed Tourist Library** series.
Birds in New Zealand is written by nine New Zealand ornithologists especially for the tourist who has not encountered New Zealand Birds before. Local birdwatchers will also find it a stimulating and useful aid to their hobby. Many colour and black and white photographs.

Birds of New Zealand in Colour

Gordon Williams

A unique collection of fifty birds native to New Zealand, from colour transparencies taken by leading nature photographers of birds in their natural habitats. With explanatory text.

New titles in this series

Common Ferns and Fern Allies

R. J. Chinnock and Eric Heath

New Zealand is renowned the world over for the abundance and variety of its fern life. Here some sixty species of fern, some of them unique to this country, are presented in full colour, with informative notes on life history, cultivation, classification and identification.

Seashore Life

R. K. Dell and Eric Heath

A useful introduction to the main groups of sea life found on our shores, from shellfish to seaweeds, sea slugs to octopi. This colourful and meticulously researched volume will be a delight to beachcomber and student alike.

Mushrooms and Toadstools

Marie Taylor

Marie Taylor's combined talents as biologist and illustrator are here brought together in this survey of some of the wide variety of mushrooms and fungi found in New Zealand's fields and woods. They range from the deadly poisonous to the eminently edible, but all are a feast for the eye, and all exemplify the extraordinary diversity of this country's rich flora.

Forthcoming titles:

Common Insects in New Zealand I and II

Annette Walker and Eric Heath

These two volumes each cover some thirty-two species of insect found around the home and in the garden, in the bush and near the shore. Accompanying each page of text are a series of beautiful and highly authoritative drawings showing the development and life cycle of the individual species, many of which are seldom recognised and little understood.

New Zealand Native Trees II

Nancy M. Adams

The long-awaited sequel to **New Zealand Native Trees I**, this volume, beautifully illustrated by the author, identifies and describes some thirty-two species of native tree found throughout New Zealand from mountain rain forest to lowland bush and scrub.

Marine Fishes

J. M. Moreland and Eric Heath

This volume describes and illustrates in colour a wide variety of the sea-fish likely to be taken in New Zealand waters. With each illustration goes the species' common, Maori and scientific names, a list of habitats and salient characteristics, diet and method of catching. An angler's and cook's delight!